Word Wise

Short Vowel Pattern VCCV

15 min.

You will need

- Teacher-made word cards
- Letter tiles
- paper
- pencil

● Choose four word cards from those provided by your teacher. Use the Letter Tiles to spell the words. Write a sentence for each of the words.

▲ Choose six word cards from those provided by your teacher. Use the Letter Tiles to spell the words. Write a sentence for each word.

■ Choose eight word cards from those provided by your teacher. Use the Letter Tiles to spell each word. Write sentences using the words.

Word Wise

Suffixes *-ful*, *-ly*, and *-ion*

15 min.

You will need

- Teacher-made word cards
- paper
- pencils

● Choose five word cards from those provided by your teacher. Write the words. Circle each word's base word. Write sentences using each word. Add other words you know with these suffixes to the list.

▲ Choose seven word cards from those provided by your teacher and write the words. Circle the base word in each word. Write sentences for each of your words. Add other words with these suffixes to the list.

■ Choose seven word cards from those provided by your teacher and write the words. Write each word's base word. Write sentences for base words and words with suffixes that show how suffixes change meanings.

Word Wise

Short Vowel Pattern VCCV

15 min.

You will need
- Teacher-made word cards
- paper
- pencil

● Choose four word cards from those provided by your teacher. Write the words. Circle the short vowels in each word. Write sentences using the words.

▲ Choose six word cards from those provided by your teacher and write the words. Circle the short vowels in each word. Write sentences using the words.

■ Choose eight word cards from those provided by your teacher and write the words. Circle the short vowels in each word. Write sentences using the words. Add other words with two syllables and short vowels to your list.

Grade 4, Unit 1, Week 2

Word Wise

Suffixes *-ess*, *-ment*, and *-ness*

15 min.

You will need
- Teacher-made word cards
- paper
- pencils

● Choose five word cards from those provided by your teacher. Write the words. Circle each word's base word. Write sentences using each word. Add other words you know with these suffixes to the list.

▲ Choose seven word cards from those provided by your teacher and write the words. Circle the base word in each word. Write sentences for each word. Add other words you know with these suffixes to the list.

■ Choose seven word cards from those provided by your teacher and write the words. Write each word's base word. Write sentences for the base words and for the words with suffixes that show how suffixes change word meanings.

Word Wise

Words with Long *a* and Long *i*

15 min.

You will need
- Teacher-made word cards • paper • pencil

● Choose four word cards from those provided by your teacher. Write the words. Circle the letter or letters that spell the long *a* or long *i* in each word. Write a sentence for each word.

▲ Choose six word cards from those provided by your teacher and write the words. Circle the letter or letters that spell the long *a* or long *i* in each word. Write a sentence for each word.

■ Choose eight word cards from those provided by your teacher and write the words in a list. Circle the letter or letters that spell the long *a* or long *i* in each word. Write a sentence for each word.

Word Wise

Prefixes *mis-*, *non-*, and *re-*

15 min.

You will need
- Teacher-made word cards
- paper
- pencils

● Choose six word cards from those provided by your teacher. Write the words. Circle the base word in each word. Write sentences using each of your words. Add other words with these prefixes to your list.

▲ Choose eight word cards from those provided by your teacher. Write the words. Circle the base word in each word. Write a sentence for each word. Add other words with these prefixes.

■ Choose eight word cards from those provided by your teacher and write the words. Write each word's base word. Write sentences for the base words and for the words with prefixes that show the different meanings.

Grade 4, Unit 6, Week 3

Word Wise

Words with Long *e* and Long *o*

You will need

15 min.

- Teacher-made word cards • paper • pencil

● Choose three word cards from those provided by your teacher with a long *e* vowel and three with a long *o* vowel. Write your words. Write a sentence for each word. Add other words with long *e* and long *o* to your list.

▲ Choose five word cards from those provided by your teacher with a long *e* vowel and five with a long *o* vowel. Write your words. Write a sentence for each word. Add other words you know with these sounds to your list.

■ Choose seven word cards from those provided by your teacher and write your words. Write sentences using your words. Add other words with these long vowel sounds to your list.

Schwa

You will need

15 min.

- Teacher-made word cards   • paper   • pencils

● Choose five word cards from those provided by your teacher. Write the words. Circle the letter or letters that form the schwa sound in each word. Write sentences using each word.

▲ Choose seven word cards from those provided by your teacher and write the words. Circle the letter or letters that form the schwa sound in each word. Write sentences using each word.

■ Choose nine word cards from those provided by your teacher and write the words. Circle the letter or letters that form the schwa sound in each word. Write sentences using each word.

Word Wise

Words with Long e

15 min.

You will need

- Teacher-made word cards
- paper
- pencil

● Choose five word cards from those provided by your teacher. Write your words. Circle the letters that spell the long *e*. Write a sentence for each word. Add other words with these long *e* spellings to the list.

▲ Choose seven word cards from those provided by your teacher and write your words. Circle the letters that spell the long *e*. Write sentences for the words. Add other words with these long *e* spellings to the list.

■ Choose ten word cards from those provided by your teacher and write the words in a list. Circle the letters that spell the long *e*. Write sentences for the words. Add other words you know with these long *e* spellings to the list.

Word Wise

Related Words

15 min.

You will need
- Teacher-made word cards
- paper
- pencils

● Choose three pairs of related word cards from those provided by your teacher. Write the words. Write sentences for each pair that show related meanings. Add other words that are related to these words.

▲ Choose four pairs of related word cards from those provided by your teacher and write the words. Write sentences for each pair that show the related meanings. Add other words to your list that are related to these words.

■ Choose five pairs of related word cards from those provided by your teacher and write the words. Write sentences for each pair that show the related meanings. Add other words that are related to these words.

Word Wise

Words with Long *u*

15 min.

You will need
- Teacher-made word cards
- paper
- pencils

● Choose five word cards from those provided by your teacher. Write your words. Write a sentence for each of your words. Think of other words you know with long *u*. Add the words to your list.

▲ Choose seven word cards from those provided by your teacher and write your words. Write a sentence for each of the words. Add other words you know with long *u* vowels to your list.

■ Choose nine word cards from those provided by your teacher and write your words. Write a sentence for each word. Add other words you know with long *u* vowels to your list.

Word Wise

Consonant Digraph /sh/

15 min.

You will need
- Teacher-made word cards
- paper
- pencils

● Choose five word cards from those provided by your teacher. List the words. Write a sentence for each of the words. Think of other words with similar spellings. Add them to your list.

▲ Choose seven word cards from those provided by your teacher and write the words in a list. Write a sentence for each of the words. Add other words with similar spellings to your list.

■ Choose nine word cards from those provided by your teacher and write the words in a list. Write sentences using the words. Add other words with similar spellings to your list.

Grade 4, Unit 5, Week 5

Word Wise

Words with -s -es or -ies

You will need
- Teacher-made word cards
- paper
- pencils

15 min.

● Choose five word cards from those provided by your teacher. Write the words. Circle the letters that make each word plural. Write a sentence using each word.

▲ Choose seven word cards from those provided by your teacher and write the words. Circle the letters that make each word plural. Write sentences using the words.

■ Choose nine word cards from those provided by your teacher and write the words. Circle the letters that make each word plural. Write sentences using the words.

Word Wise

Endings *-er* and *-ar*

15 min.

You will need
- Teacher-made word cards
- paper
- pencils

● Choose five word cards from those provided by your teacher. List your words. Write a sentence for each of the words. Think of other words that have these endings. Add them to your list.

▲ Choose seven word cards from those provided by your teacher and write your words in a list. Write a sentence for each of the words. Add other words to your list that have these endings.

■ Choose ten word cards from those provided by your teacher and write your words in a list. Write sentences using the words. Add other words to your list that have these endings.

Word Wise

Irregular Plurals

15 min.

You will need
- Teacher-made word cards
- paper
- pencils

● Choose five word cards from those provided by your teacher. Write the words. Circle the letters that make each word plural. Write a sentence using each word.

▲ Choose seven word cards from those provided by your teacher and write the words. Circle the letters that make each word plural. Write sentences using the words.

■ Choose nine word cards from those provided by your teacher and write the words. Circle the letters that make each word plural. Write sentences using the words.

Word Wise

Final Syllable Patterns

15 min.

You will need
- Teacher-made word cards
- paper
- pencils

● Choose five word cards from those provided by your teacher. List the words. Circle the final syllable in each word. Write a sentence for each. Add other words with these final syllables to your list.

▲ Choose seven word cards from those provided by your teacher and list the words. Circle the final syllable in each word. Write sentences using the words. Add other words to the list with these final syllables.

■ Choose nine word cards from those provided by your teacher and list the words. Circle the final syllable in each word. Write sentences using the words. Add other words to the list with these final syllables.

Word Wise

Words with *ar* and *or*

You will need

15 min.

• Teacher-made word cards   • paper   • pencils

● Choose six word cards from those provided by your teacher. Write the words. Write sentences using each of the words. Add other words you know with *ar* or *or* to your list.

▲ Choose eight word cards from those provided by your teacher and write the words. Write sentences using each of the words. Add other words with *ar* or *or* to your list.

■ Choose ten word cards from those provided by your teacher and write the words. Add other words with *ar* or *or* to your list. Write a short paragraph that tells a story. Try to use all of the words.

Word Wise

Multisyllabic Words

15 min.

You will need
- Teacher-made word cards
- paper
- pencils

● Choose four word cards from those provided by your teacher. Write the words and the number of syllables in the words. Write sentences using each word.

▲ Choose six word cards from those provided by your teacher and write the words. Write the number of syllables in each word. Write sentences using each word.

■ Choose eight word cards from those provided by your teacher and write the words. Next to each word, write the number of syllables in the word. Write sentences using each word.

Consonant Pairs *ng, nk, ph,*

15 min.

You will need
- Teacher-made word cards
- paper
- pencils

● Choose five word cards from those provided by your teacher. Write the words in a list. Circle the consonant pair in each word. Write sentences using your words. Add other words you know with consonant pairs to your list.

▲ Choose six word cards from those provided by your teacher and write the words in a list. Circle the consonant pair in each word and write sentences using the words. Add other words with consonant pairs to your list.

■ Choose eight word cards from those provided by your teacher and write your words in a list. Add other words with consonant pairs to the list. Write a poem using some of the words.

Prefixes *un-*, *dis-*, and *in-*

15 min.

You will need

- Teacher-made word cards
- paper
- pencils

● Choose two word cards from those provided by your teacher with each prefix: *un-*, *dis-* and *in-*. Write the words. Write a sentence for each word. Think of other words with these prefixes. Add them to your list.

▲ Choose three word cards from those provided by your teacher with each prefix: *un-*, *dis-* and *in-*. Write the words. Write sentences using each word. Add other words with these prefixes to your list.

■ Choose four word cards from those provided by your teacher with prefixes *un-*, *dis-* and *in-*. Write the words. Write sentences using each word and add other words with these prefixes to your list.

Word Wise

Words with *-ear, -ir, -our,* and *-ur*

You will need
15 min.

- Teacher-made word cards • paper • pencils

● Choose at least one word card from those provided by your teacher with each letter combination *-ear, -ir, -our,* and *-ur*. Write the words in a list. Write a sentence for each of the words.

▲ Choose two word cards from those provided by your teacher with each of the letter combinations: *-ear, -ir, -our,* and *-ur*. Write the words in a list. Write a sentence for each of the words.

■ Choose three word cards from those provided by your teacher with each letter combination: *-ear, -ir, -our,* and *-ur*. Write the words in a list. Use each word in a sentence. Add other words with these combinations to the list.

Consonant Digraph /sh/

15 min.

You will need

- Teacher-made word cards
- paper
- pencils

● Choose five word cards from those provided by your teacher. List the words. Write a sentence for each of the words. Think of other words with similar spellings. Add them to your list.

▲ Choose seven word cards from those provided by your teacher and write the words in a list. Write a sentence for each of the words. Add other words with similar spellings to your list.

■ Choose nine word cards from those provided by your teacher and write the words in a list. Write sentences using the words. Add other words with similar spellings to your list.

Word Wise

Words with *-ed* and *-ing*

15 min.

You will need
- Teacher-made word cards
- paper
- pencils

● Choose five word cards from those provided by your teacher. List the words. Circle each word's base word. Write a sentence for each word. Add other words to your list with *-ed* and *-ing*.

▲ Choose seven word cards from those provided by your teacher. List the words. Circle each word's base word. Write sentences using the words. Add other words with *-ed* and *-ing*.

■ Choose ten word cards from those provided by your teacher and write the words in a list. Circle each word's base word. Then write sentences using the words. Add other words to your list with *-ed* and *-ing*.

Word Wise

Endings *-er* and *-ar*

15 min.

You will need
- Teacher-made word cards
- paper
- pencils

● Choose five word cards from those provided by your teacher. List your words. Write a sentence for each of the words. Think of other words that have these endings. Add them to your list.

▲ Choose seven word cards from those provided by your teacher and write your words in a list. Write a sentence for each of the words. Add other words to your list that have these endings.

■ Choose ten word cards from those provided by your teacher and write your words in a list. Write sentences using the words. Add other words to your list that have these endings.

Grade 4, Unit 4, Week 4

Word Wise

Homophones

15 min.

You will need

- Teacher-made word cards
- paper
- pencils

● Choose three pairs of homophones from the word cards provided by your teacher. List the words. Write a sentence for each word that shows the different spellings and meanings.

▲ Choose four pairs of homophones from the word cards provided by your teacher. List the words. Write sentences for each pair that show their different spellings and meanings.

■ Choose six word cards from those provided by your teacher and list the words. Next to each word write a homophone. Write sentences for each pair of homophones.

Word Wise

Final Syllable Patterns

15 min.

You will need

- Teacher-made word cards
- paper
- pencils

● Choose five word cards from those provided by your teacher. List the words. Circle the final syllable in each word. Write a sentence for each. Add other words with these final syllables to your list.

▲ Choose seven word cards from those provided by your teacher and list the words. Circle the final syllable in each word. Write sentences using the words. Add other words to the list with these final syllables.

■ Choose nine word cards from those provided by your teacher and list the words. Circle the final syllable in each word. Write sentences using the words. Add other words to the list with these final syllables.

Word Wise

Vowel Sound in *Shout*

15 min.

You will need

- Teacher-made word cards
- paper
- pencils

● Choose five word cards from those provided by your teacher. List the words. Circle the letters that form the sound /ou/ as in the word *shout* in each word. Write sentences using each word. Add other words with this sound.

▲ Choose seven word cards from those provided by your teacher and list the words. Circle the letters that form the sound /ou/ as in the word *shout*. Write sentences using the words. Add other words with this sound.

■ Choose ten word cards from those provided by your teacher. Make a two-column chart with the headings *ou* and *ow*. List words in the correct columns and write a sentence using each word. Add more words to your chart.

Word Wise

Contractions

You will need

15 min.

- Teacher-made word cards
- paper
- pencils

● Choose four word cards from those provided by your teacher. Write the words in a list. Write sentences using each of your words. Next to each contraction, write the two words that form the contraction.

▲ Choose six word cards from those provided by your teacher and list the words. Write sentences using each word. Next to each contraction, write the two words that form it.

■ Choose eight word cards from those provided by your teacher and list the words. Write sentences using each word. Next to each contraction, write the two words that form it.

Word Wise

Compound Words

You will need

15 min.

- Teacher-made word cards
- paper
- pencils

● Choose five word cards from those provided by your teacher. List your words. Circle the two words that form the compound word. Write sentences using each of the compound words. Add other compound words to the list.

▲ Choose eight word cards from those provided by your teacher and list your words. Circle the two words that form the compound word. Write sentences using each of the compound words.

■ Choose ten word cards from those provided by your teacher and list your words. Next to each compound word, write the two words that form it. Write sentences using each compound word.

Word Wise

Possessives

You will need

15 min.

- Teacher-made word cards
- paper
- pencils

● Choose five word cards from those provided by your teacher. List the words. Circle the possessive in each word. Write sentences using each word. Add other possessive words to your list.

▲ Choose seven word cards from those provided by your teacher. List the words. Circle the possessive in each word. Write sentences using each word. Add other examples of possessive words to your list.

■ Choose seven word cards from those provided by your teacher. List the words. Circle the possessive in each word. Write sentences for each word. Write a list of the base words without the possessive form.

Grade 4, Unit 4, Week 1